Houdini

SADDLEBACK
EDUCATIONAL PUBLISHING

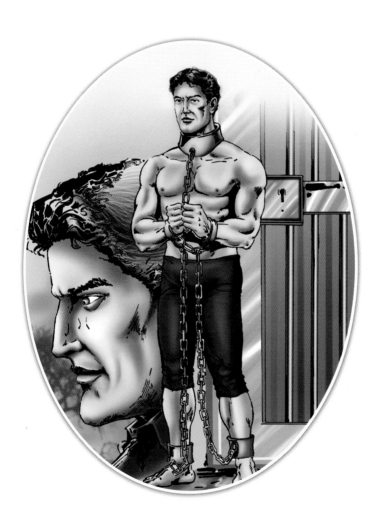

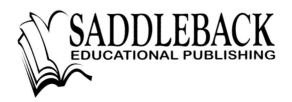

Saddleback's Graphic Biographies

ISBN-13: 978-1-59905-224-3
ISBN-10: 1-59905-224-5
eBook: 978-1-60291-587-9

Printed in Guangzhou, China
1011/CA21101634

15 14 13 12 11 3 4 5 6 7 8 9

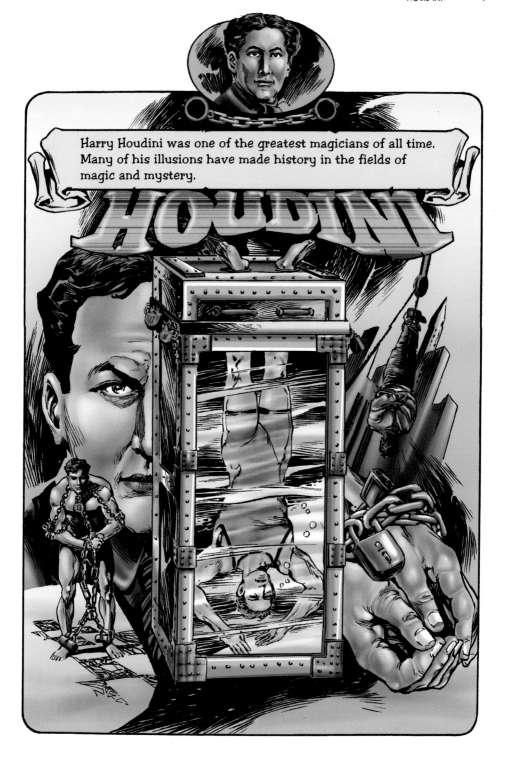

Harry Houdini was one of the greatest magicians of all time. Many of his illusions have made history in the fields of magic and mystery.

2

Harry Houdini was born Ehrich Weiss, the son of Samuel and Cecilia Weiss, on March 24, 1874, in Budapest, Hungary. But soon after, the family moved to Appleton, Wisconsin, where Samuel became the town's first rabbi. The family spelled Ehrich's name a new way: Erich.

Your husband is a fine rabbi, Mrs. Weiss, but why won't he learn English?

Samuel is a proud man, and old-fashioned, I'm afraid.

Samuel moved his family to a new land but he never learned to accept new ways.

Young Erich was not like most babies.

Ah, my little son, you never cry. And day or night I always find you wide eyed and awake.

Several years later, Samuel lost his job and the family moved to Milwaukee.

We are sorry, Rabbi, but you are old-fashioned.

Thank you for your kindness. We'll get by.

The family had a hard time getting enough money for food. Young Erich and his brothers helped in any way that they could.

Extra! Extra! Read all about it!

But young Erich was always thinking of new things to do. At the age of nine he gave his first show.

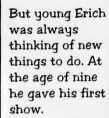

Step right up. Only five cents. See young Erich— Prince of the Air!

At the age of twelve, Erich decided to run away from home and find a regular job to help the family. As usual, he thought of something that not many other boys had tried.

Can I come along?

Sure, there's plenty of boots to be shined here.

But this job didn't last long. Erich soon found himself moving from town to town to find work.

This one's postmarked Hanibal, Missouri.

What! Oh, thank you!

The Weiss family was never sure where Erich would turn up next.

Dear Ma,
I'm going to Galveston, Texas and will be home in about a year.
My best regards to all.
Your truant son,
Erich Weiss

To:
Mrs. C. Weiss,
517 6th St.,
Milwaukee,
Wisconsin

But Erich always wrote. And he sent money whenever he could.

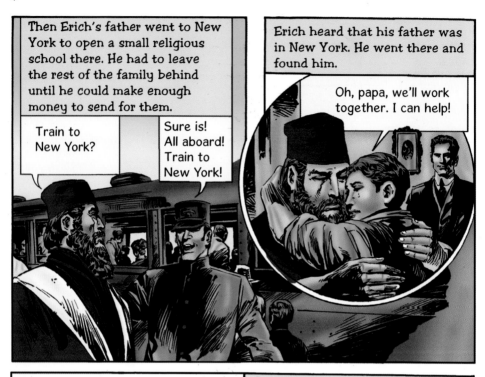

Then Erich's father went to New York to open a small religious school there. He had to leave the rest of the family behind until he could make enough money to send for them.

Train to New York?

Sure is! All aboard! Train to New York!

Erich heard that his father was in New York. He went there and found him.

Oh, papa, we'll work together. I can help!

Soon they earned enough money to send for the rest of the family.

Erich, my son.

Oh, Mama!

But things were not easy. It was hard for Rabbi Weiss to earn enough money to support his family. Erich and his brother helped as much as they could.

The Lord will provide. The Lord will provide

Rabbi Weiss was a very religious man.

Erich was working as a messenger for a department store. He had an idea.

It's the holiday season. This should work.

Christmas is coming. Turkeys are fat. Please drop a quarter in the Messenger Boy's hat.

Erich's plan worked even better than he thought it would.

That evening he put the coins up his sleeves, behind his ears, and in his hair. When his mother opened the door ...

Shake me, I'm magic!

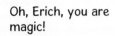

Oh, Erich, you are magic!

Now the holidays looked much brighter.

About this time Erich's younger brother showed him a simple coin trick.

Now you see it.

Now you don't.

Soon, Erich was reading everything he could get his hands on about magic.

You should go to sleep, you must get up early.

In a minute, Mother.

But none of the jobs lasted long. Again he needed a job, but he knew he wouldn't stand a chance with the other boys that were waiting. He had read that a magician needs to believe in himself. Perhaps it would work here too!

Thank you for waiting, but I'm afraid that this job is already taken.

It worked. The other boys walked away.

I want this job.

It looks like you've got it.

On weekends, Erich ran with the Pastime Athletic Club track team. For the rest for his life he kept himself in good physical condition.

Good time, Erich!

His father was against tobacco and alcohol for religious reasons. Erich's coach was against them because he felt they slowed up the body as well as the soul.

He read many books on magic. He gave neighborhood shows as his skill blossomed.

Then he chanced on a book by a great French magician.

If I could only become like Robert-Houdin.

MEMOIRS OF ROBERT HOUDIN

One day at lunch a friend had a suggestion.

Houdini!

All you have to do to be "like Houdin" is to add an "i" to the end of his name.

And so, at seventeen, Erich Weiss became "Harry Houdini." His brother Theo was his partner. They got their first chance at a theater in New York. It was because the regular act didn't appear.

As you see, he is securely locked.

And the box is chained closed.

Now I will clap my hands together three times—and behold! A miracle!

But no miracle took place. Instead, after a long wait, the curtains closed and the band played the music for the next act. Harry found that his brother was still a prisoner.

What happened!

I left the keys in the dressing room!

The act was fired on the spot.

You guys don't know what you're doing! Try the dime museums!

And so the "Brothers Houdini" left town to tour the Midwest. They made certain changes in the act.

Behold a miracle.

After this first failure, Harry was always the one to be tied and locked in the box. They gained experience and skill, but the salaries were low. Often they had to work as many as twenty shows in one day.

It was a hard life. For years young Houdini struggled. But one day he found a new kind of magic.

Who is that young girl?

That's Bessie Rahner.

It was love at first sight.

You amaze me.

Well then, let's do a disappearing act and get married.

And so they did. They ran away and were married by a Justice of the Peace. Bess' family was Catholic and Harry's was Jewish. To make their families happy, they were later married again by both a priest and then a rabbi.

Why, I'm the most married person I know, three times—and to the same man!

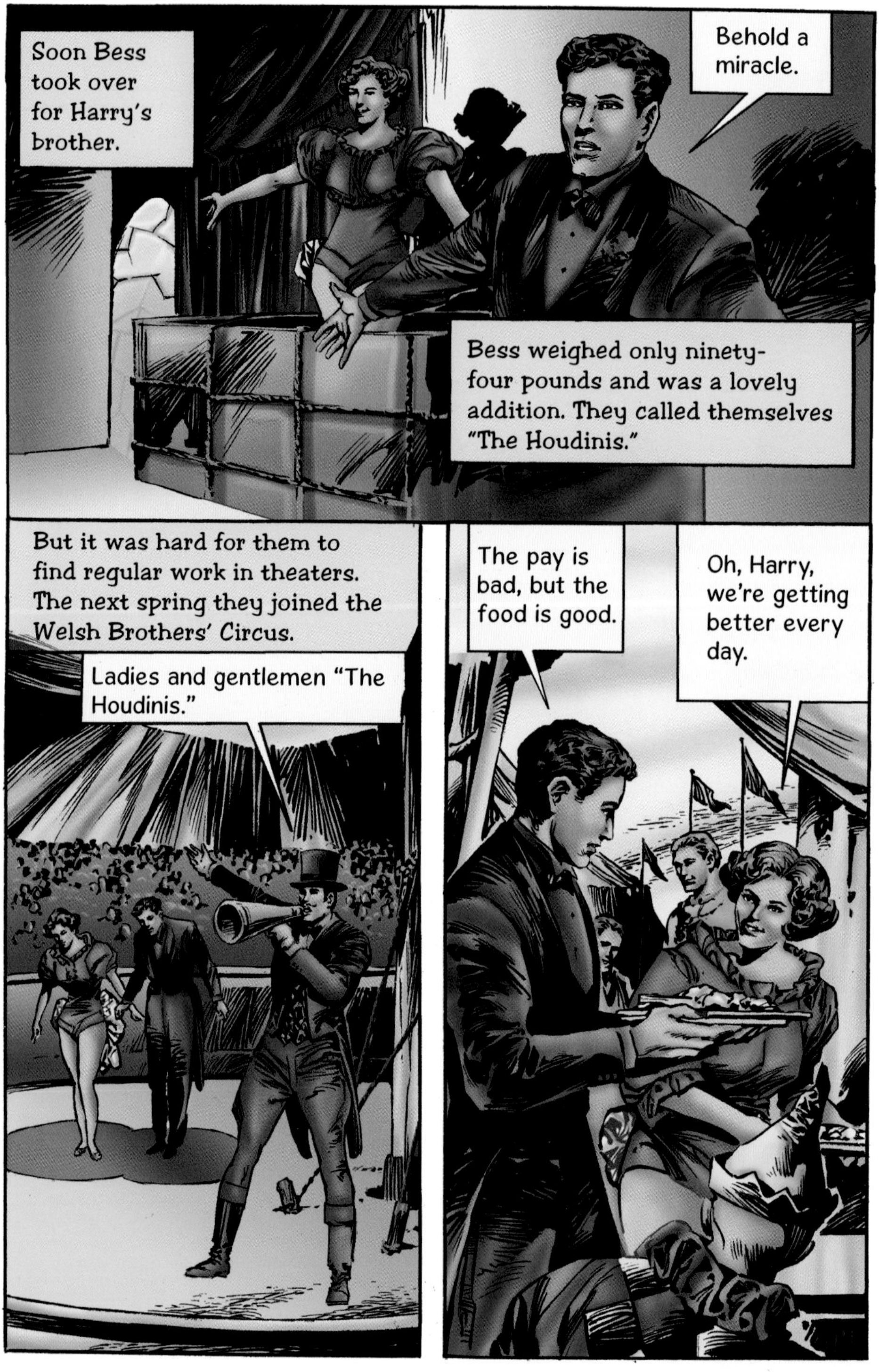
Soon Bess took over for Harry's brother.
Behold a miracle.
Bess weighed only ninety-four pounds and was a lovely addition. They called themselves "The Houdinis."
But it was hard for them to find regular work in theaters. The next spring they joined the Welsh Brothers' Circus.
Ladies and gentlemen "The Houdinis."
The pay is bad, but the food is good.
Oh, Harry, we're getting better every day.

About this time Houdini became interested in handcuffs.

I can open them with a tiny piece of wire.

Practice makes perfect!

The next summer, Houdini tried his first publicity stunt while on tour in Nova Scotia, Canada.

As you see, Houdini is tied to the back of a wild stallion. Can he escape?

Unfortunately the horse was wilder than he thought.

Stop! Stop!

Miles away the tired horse stopped, and Houdini escaped from his bonds.

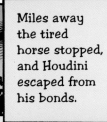

Too bad no one was around to see my escape!

In 1897 the Houdinis toured the Midwest with a medicine show.

First the Houdinis and other acts would draw a crowd. Then Dr. Hill would appear and sell his medicine.

At this time, many spirit mediums who said they could speak with ghosts were also giving shows.

But Dr. Hill wanted to cash in on the large audience crowds that came for "spirit shows."

These spiritualists are all fakes! Their tricks are easy compared to what we do.

SUNDAY SPIRIT SHOW
HEAR MESSAGES FROM THE DEAD.
KANSAS CITY
MAR. 19th 8 P.M.
GRAND HALL

I'll give you top billing and a raise if you'll do a Sunday spirit show.

That will be easy for a magician.

They were successful, but Houdini disliked the spirit show. He was an entertainer and showman, not a cheat. The next summer he and Bess returned to the circus.

I promise if we don't make the big time in one year, I'll quit show business.

In St. Paul, Minnesota, Houdini met Martin Beck. Beck hired acts for vaudeville theaters.

I like your act, but I want you to get rid of magic tricks and work on your escape routines.

Beck got the Houdinis a job at the Orpheum Theater in Omaha for sixty dollars a week—the highest salary they had ever received.

Now watch the impossible made possible.

Houdini escaped from five pair of official handcuffs supplied by the Omaha police. He was a hit. Beck signed Houdini for a tour.

About that time a San Francisco newspaper ran a story that said Houdini's escapes didn't take much skill. They said that he used keys that were hidden in his clothes.

Now we'll chain you to this chair and lock the closet.

So during a visit to San Francisco, Houdini challenged the police. And they made sure that he had no hidden keys.

In ten minutes he was free from the closet.

It was a sensation. Houdini's salary soared. The newspaper ran a story which said they were wrong about the hidden keys.

SAN FRANCISCO HERALD

ESCAPE KING OUTDOES POLICE

Overnight he was a hit. Soon he was the star of vaudeville shows in every city. He escaped from police handcuffs and jail cells all over the country.

Amidst this new success, Houdini decided to sail for England on May 30, 1900. Vaudeville was even bigger in Europe at that time, and Houdini was headed for the top.

His first stop was Scotland Yard. He put on a show for the officers.

Have you any others? Easy as pie!

When he opened at the Alhambra Theater in London in July, he was a smash hit. They kept him there until the end of August.

Any other challengers?

Houdini invited anyone to bring their own handcuffs for him to escape from. He easily escaped from them all.

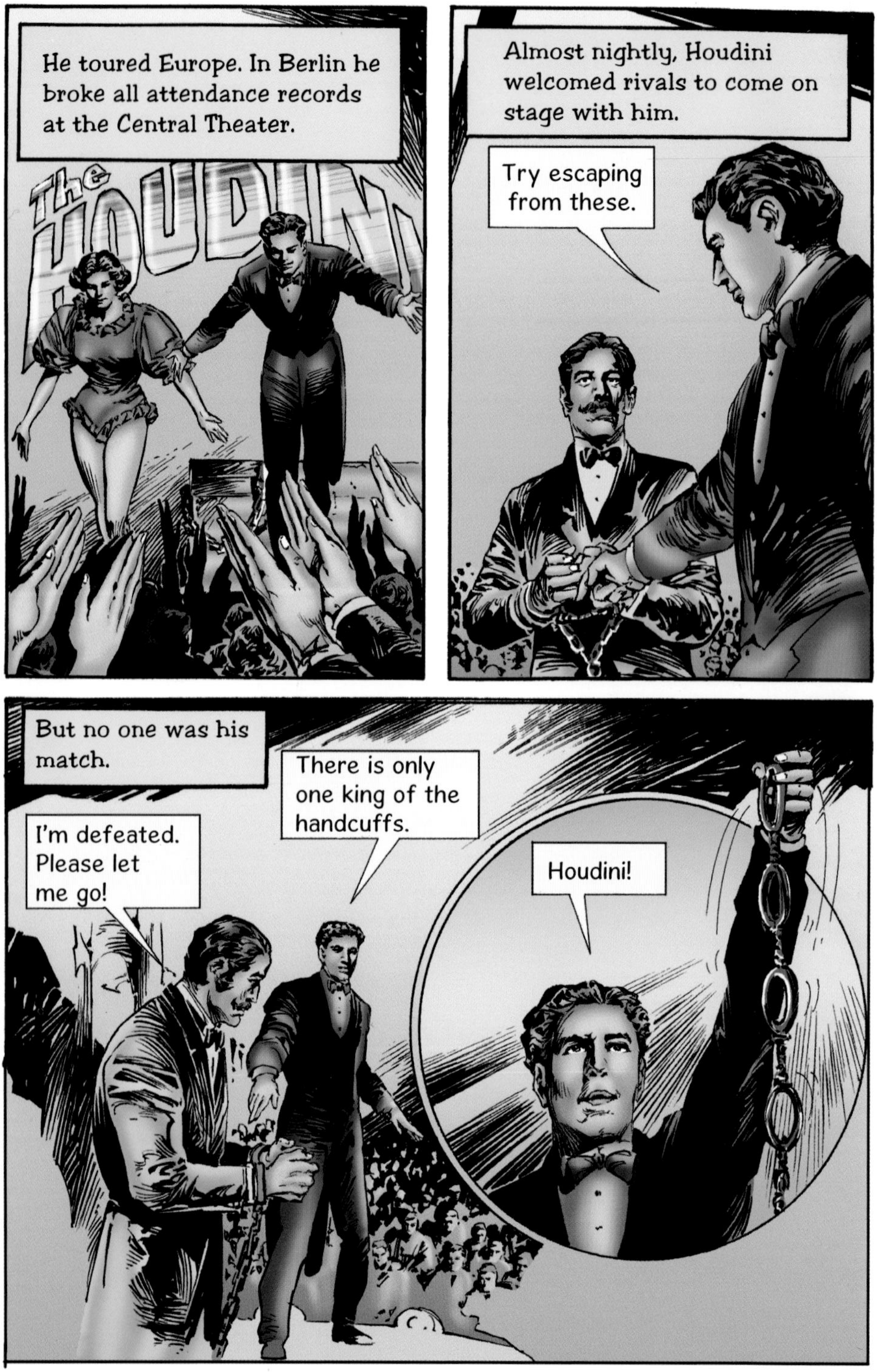
He toured Europe. In Berlin he broke all attendance records at the Central Theater.
The HOUDINI
Almost nightly, Houdini welcomed rivals to come on stage with him.
Try escaping from these.
But no one was his match.
I'm defeated. Please let me go!
There is only one king of the handcuffs.
Houdini!

The Dutch windmills gave Houdini a wild idea. He was strapped to an arm of a windmill.

The arm broke, and he fell to the ground.

Fortunately, Houdini was unhurt and the publicity packed the theaters he played at for many weeks.

He toured Russia, where he was asked to give a private show at the Kleinmichel Palace for the Grand Duke.

When he returned to England, there were riots for tickets wherever he played. He was the most popular vaudeville star in history.

Finally Houdini decided to return to the United States.

We've been gone for five years.

I wonder how Americans will receive you now.

It was tremendous. Sold out!

On January 5, 1906, he got national press coverage when he entered the United States jail in Washington D.C.

Most of his clothes were taken away, and he was searched and handcuffed. Then Houdini was locked in the cell that had held the man who assassinated President Garfield.

In two minutes he was free. Then he decided to play a wild trick.

What are you doing?

In twenty-seven minutes he unlocked all the cells on "Murderers' Row" and moved the convicts around.

With such great publicity stunts, Houdini was a success everywhere.

In some cities he jumped handcuffed from a bridge while thousands watched.

He's free. He's free.

Quick, let's go buy tickets for tonight's show!

The climax of his stage act was escaping from a padlocked-can filled with water.

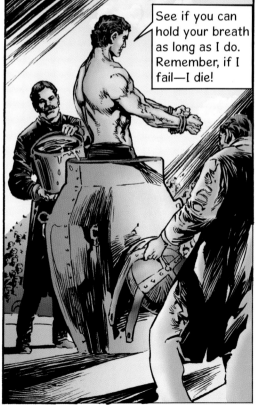

See if you can hold your breath as long as I do. Remember, if I fail—I die!

No one could hold their breath as long as Houdini.

He toured the world. In Australia in 1910, he was the first man to fly a plane over that continent.

He had first learned to fly one year before. But after leaving Australia he never flew again.

Everywhere he went he visited the graves of great magicians.

His family is too poor to keep up this grave. I will start a fund to help out.

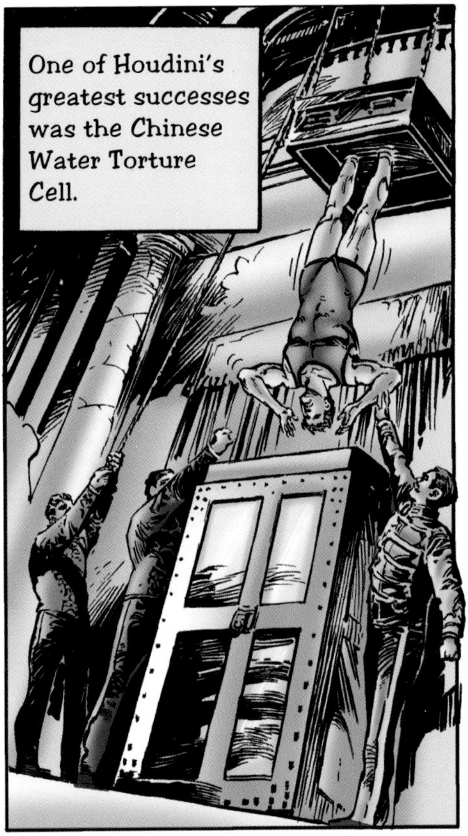
One of Houdini's greatest successes was the Chinese Water Torture Cell.

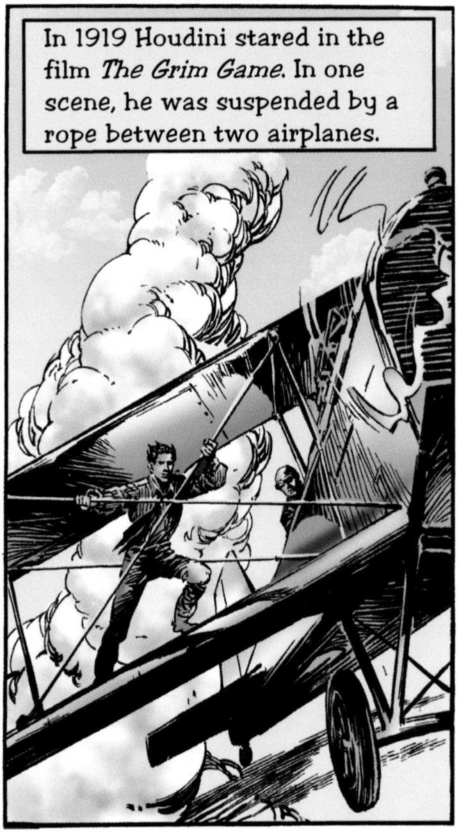
In 1919 Houdini stared in the film *The Grim Game*. In one scene, he was suspended by a rope between two airplanes.

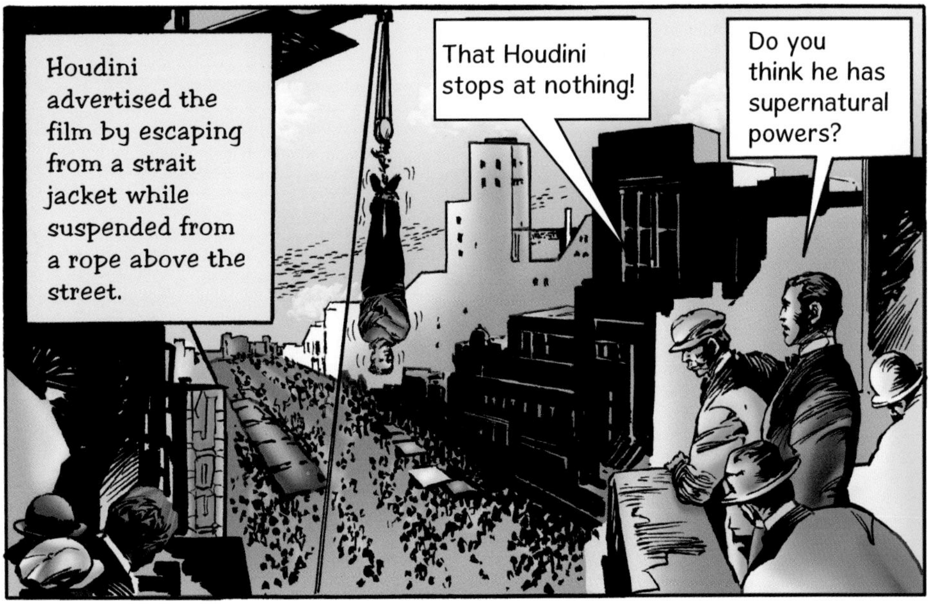
Houdini advertised the film by escaping from a strait jacket while suspended from a rope above the street.
That Houdini stops at nothing!
Do you think he has supernatural powers?

In 1924 Houdini began a crusade against "spiritualism." He toured the United States exposing the so-called spiritualists who claimed to contact the dead.

Every spiritualist uses tricks like these to fool people into believing that they have special powers.

I too use tricks and have secrets, which I will never tell. But anyone here could do as I do if they knew them.

Many wondered what trick Houdini used at the New York Hippodrome.

And now ladies and gentlemen, I will draw the curtain.

For nineteen straight weeks the elephant disappeared when he fired a pistol. It was the biggest stage feat in the history of magic.

Once again, the impossible was made possible.

Many people thought the escape king could escape even death. But on Halloween of 1926 Houdini died tragically from a ruptured appendix.

NEW YORK
SECTION
KING OF MAGIC PASSES ON

The world mourned the man who had delighted and amazed it. But the magic he gave the world would make his legend grow long after he was gone.

The END

Saddleback's Graphic Fiction & Nonfiction

If you enjoyed this Graphic Biography ... you will also enjoy our other graphic titles including:

Graphic Classics

- Around the World in Eighty Days
- The Best of Poe
- Black Beauty
- The Call of the Wild
- A Christmas Carol
- A Connecticut Yankee in King Arthur's Court
- Dr. Jekyll and Mr. Hyde
- Dracula
- Frankenstein
- The Great Adventures of Sherlock Holmes
- Gulliver's Travels
- Huckleberry Finn
- The Hunchback of Notre Dame
- The Invisible Man
- Jane Eyre
- Journey to the Center of the Earth

- Kidnapped
- The Last of the Mohicans
- The Man in the Iron Mask
- Moby Dick
- The Mutiny On Board H.M.S. Bounty
- The Mysterious Island
- The Prince and the Pauper
- The Red Badge of Courage
- The Scarlet Letter
- The Swiss Family Robinson
- A Tale of Two Cities
- The Three Musketeers
- The Time Machine
- Tom Sawyer
- Treasure Island
- 20,000 Leagues Under the Sea
- The War of the Worlds

Graphic Shakespeare

- As You Like It
- Hamlet
- Julius Caesar
- King Lear
- Macbeth
- The Merchant of Venice

- A Midsummer Night's Dream
- Othello
- Romeo and Juliet
- The Taming of the Shrew
- The Tempest
- Twelfth Night

SADDLEBACK
EDUCATIONAL PUBLISHING